Reflections On Healing Our Ailing Earth

Edward Lee Amerson

Wolf Portait for cover by Leslie Macon

Copyright © 1998 by Edward Lee Amerson

All rights reserved.

No part of this book may be used or reproduced in any manner whatsoever without written permission except in the case of brief quotations embodied in critical articles and reviews.

Clip Art images published by Microstar★

ISBN: 0-9626995-1-9

Moondog Press

Wolf Portrait for front cover entitled "Moonsong" copyright © 1997 by Leslie Macon

First Edition

Printed in the United States by:
Morris Publishing · 3212 East Highway 30 · Kearney, NE 68847
Phone 1-800-650-7888

SING WITH WOLVES

"Behold my brothers, the spring has come;
The earth has received the embraces of the sun
And we shall soon see the results of that love!
Every seed is awakened and so has all animal life.
It is through this mysterious power that we too have our being
And we therefore yield to our neighbors,
Even our animal neighbors,
The same right as ourselves, to inhabit the land."

—Sitting Bull

CONTENTS

PREFACE 9

Author's Note 15
Reflections

> The Tattered Web 19
> Dreamwalking 25
> Spiritual Roots 31
> Aliens 37
> Crossroads 43
> Wilderness 49
> The Seeing Heart 55
> Earth, Wind, and Sky 63
> The Spirit Within 67
> Sacred Moments 71
> Purpose 77
> Sacred Beauty 81

EndNote 85

Index to Quotations 93

hope of having a promising future, then we must empty our minds of falsehoods of self-separateness from the natural world.

I have borrowed supportive thoughts from naturalists, John Muir, Henry David Thoreau, Wallace Stegner, Lorean Eisely, and others. I have also borrowed supportive thoughts from the Native Americans, both past and present. As I have written in this modest book, *Native Americans cannot speak of religion without relating to the mountains, trees, the sky and sun, plants and animals. Nor can they talk of nature without mentioning harmony, balance, reverence, beauty, and kinship. Nature is the embodiment of their spiritual beliefs.**

If we truly desire to halt the rampant environmental destruction that is now occurring, we of the mass consumer societies must learn to think in ways that provoke—balance, harmony, and respect for Mother Earth and all her living beings.

We must rekindle our sense of earth sacredness. For the further we journey from our earth-spirituality, the more hardened our hearts become. We must measure ourselves not by the width of our greed but by the depth of our wisdom.

Let our thoughts be wings to elevate us to higher spheres, so that we may see clearer, the landscape below, in all its colors, patterns, and intertwinings.

---

*The term *Native American* as it is used throughout this book refers both to historical Native Americans and the Native American peoples of the present who still maintain their traditional spiritual beliefs inherited from their ancestors.

Reflections On Healing Our Ailing Earth

"Why should man value himself as more than a small part of the great creation?"

—John Muir

Author's Note

For so long, we have envisioned ourselves as being separate from nature. We have denounced the fact that non-human beings have feelings just as we do. We cringe at the thought of being equal to the smallest creature. We see land *not* as a living spiritual entity but a commodity for short term personal gain.

Is it no wonder that our forests are being desecrated, our rivers polluted, our wetlands drained? Is it not surprising that just within a few decades an unprecedented number of plants and animals have become extinct or are on the edge of oblivion?

We have become so estranged from our earth-home that we behave as if we were aliens from another planet. Alien beings instead of human beings.

In our material pursuits we have orphaned ourselves from the beauty, mystery, and spirituality of the natural world around us, resulting in apathy toward the destruction of our home-planet. We have attempted to mend parts of our wounded earth

Sing with Wolves 🐾

by passing environmental laws and preserving land areas of pristine quality, hoping technology will somehow solve the rest.

However, we cannot depend solely on government regulations, technology or preservation.

The fate of earth and all its living beings is hinged upon our willingness to humble ourselves among all earth's creations.

Our planet can no longer survive the onslaught of an ego-warrior wielding a sword against her.

We must relate in ways that venture far beyond envisioning ourselves as godly creatures that are independent of nature's immutable laws.

We must come to an ancient understanding that has sustained Native Americans and other tribal cultures around the world for thousands of years—we are a mere strand in the sacred web of life.

We must understand from the depths of our being that all life, no matter how small or seemingly insignificant, is an important link in the continual spinning of the sacred web.

We must abolish our illusionary belief that we are super-beings living in a world of sub-beings.

We are at the crossroads. We must again recognize that all life has purpose and has a right to fulfill that purpose.

The fate of our home-planet is hitched to our willingness to realize that true power is not one of chest thumping, but seeing with the heart.

Like the silk threads of the orb weaver, all life is interconnected. When we wantonly destroy plants and animals, wetlands and forests we are tattering the intricate web of life.

THE TATTERED WEB

How long can man snip the strands of life's web and still survive?
—David Cavagnaro

Like the silk threads of the orb weaver, all life is interconnected. When we wantonly destroy plants and animals, wetlands and forests we are tattering the intricate web of life.

Traditional Native Americans understood this principle well. They viewed themselves as part of the web of life—not apart from it. They did not see themselves as superior beings but equal to the other animal and plant beings.

Moreover, they believed that every plant, animal, insect, reptile, fish, bird, and stone was charged with a spiritual power that created all things—they felt a deep kinship with all creation.

Chief Luther Standing Bear—*Kinship with all creatures of the earth, sky, and water was a real and active principle. For the animal and the bird world there existed a brotherly feeling that kept the Lakota safe among them and so close did some of the Lakotas come to their feathered and furred friends that in*

Sing with Wolves

true brotherhood they spoke a common tonque. The old Lakota was wise. He knew that lack of respect for growing, living things soon led to lack of respect for humans too.

The Native Americans understood that all things are not divided from each other but intertwined and interdependent. They understood that survival is not based on the fittest but mutual cooperation.

A bee cannot survive without the flower and the flower without the bee.

This is nature's mandate.

We cannot detach ourselves from the sacred web of life without violating Mother Nature's law of mutual cooperation.

And yet, we of the industrialized nations are doing just that—we are destroying the woven threads that interlinks all life to each other.

We have been fooled into thinking that we are somehow outside the web. *Super-beings.*

Scientists have been warning us of the dangers of global warming, habitat destruction, species extinction. All of which are due to our false sense of separateness from the world around us.

We can no longer view nature as something outside ourselves, something created by a deity to serve our needs. Now we must give birth to an ancient paradigm—all living beings are tethered to each other.

Sing with Wolves)

Alex Jacobs, Iroquois—*To us each object is imbued with invisible fibers of light that reach out into the universe and are connected and related to all things and all times, and the song that the maker sang when making the object still hangs in the air.*

The invisible fibers of light is the thread that connects us to the jaguar, to the osprey, the antelope, to the common earthworm, the mussel, and the stars. If we continue to believe in the myth that we are somehow separate from nature, then we must ponder if, we too, will come the way of the ivory billed woodpecker, the passenger pigeon, and the snow leopard—all of which have vanished due to our arrogant attitude toward Mother Earth.

If we are to survive into the next millennium, then we must restore our sense of kinship with all life.

Only when we begin to see ourselves as part of the great mystery can we begin to mend those parts of the web that we have weakened.

We must rid ourselves of the notion that we are super-beings living in a world of sub-beings on a planet with infinite resources.

We can no longer afford to turn whole forests into toothpicks and toilet paper, wetlands into parking lots, and oceans into chemical cocktails, our deserts into nuclear waste dumps.

If life is to continue in all its beauty, complexity and wonder, then we must not only change our attitudes as to who we are on planet earth but toward all life on earth. Our survival and the survival of future generations of people, plants, animals, the scaly ones, and those with wings are dependent on the way,we, the Super-beings, view ourselves in the living web of life.

Sing with Wolves I

Aldo Leopold—*We know now what was unknown to all preceding caravan of generations: that men are only fellow-voyagers with other living creatures in the odyssey of evolution. This new knowledge* **should have** *given us, by this time, a sense of kinship with other fellow creatures: a wish to live and let live: a sense of wonder over the magnitude and duration of the biotic enterprise.*

I emphasized *should have* in the above passage because as Leopold understood, we have not yet grasped the idea that we are all *fellow voyagers with other living creatures in the odyssey of evolution.*

If our odyssey is to continue then we must once again recognize that all things are bonded in the sacred web of life. If we break the bonds of the web, then the web unravels and life, as we know it, will cease to be.

Every day a miracle unfolds, in caterpillars becoming butterflies, tadpoles into frogs, nymphs into mayflies, starlight into matter.

DREAMWALKING

"No synonym for God is as perfect as beauty"
—John Muir

Our earth-home is bursting with beauty, brimming with magic, overflowing with miracles—yet we all seem to be dreamwalking.

How rare it is to find ourselves staring deeply into the heart of a flower, or listening to the notes of the song bird, or embracing a fiery sunrise.

It is as if we have lost our capacity to see, to hear, and feel. How can we live on a miracle planet and not get rhapsodic? Have our eyes grown weary of the beauty, our ears deaf to the song of life?

Everyday a miracle unfolds, in caterpillars becoming butterflies, tadpoles into frogs, nymphs into mayflies, and starlight into matter.

We become bewitched by the possibility of life on Mars, yet, the beauty of life about us goes unseen. In our dream-state we care very little about the welfare of our home-planet. Even

Sing with Wolves

when we witness fish floating bottom-up with tumors on their sides, frogs being born with legs on their backs, or bloated dolphins ebbing at the shoreline, there is still no compassion for our ailing planet.

Perhaps the reason for our stupor is because earth's pain is too unbearable. One of the sorrows of loving earth is that one feels her pain. So we dreamwalk to avoid suffering; we dreamwalk to avoid responsibility.

But as we belatedly awaken, the panda bear and rhino, manatee and the panther, the woodland caribou, the key deer, and the jaguar, along with the ocelot, and the prairie dog, the red wolf and the whooping crane will all have vanished.

Being born on this wondrous planet is not a bum deal; it is a celebration. Life as we know it is a one-time opportunity. Yet we are not celebrating.

If we could only awake from our dreamwalk and see, once again, the beauty of creation around us, then we would dance joyfully in the sunset of each evening and rise early to meet the morning star.

We would walk as friends with the animal beings—we would talk to them and listen to what they had to say. Our souls would be a raging river of compassion for all life; we would run through tall grass meadows and sing with wolves and leap like deer.

We can no longer afford to dreamwalk through life; it is time to awaken from our slumber and see once again with our awakening hearts—the daily beauty of life around us.

Beauty is everywhere. There is beauty in bending light on polished stone; there is beauty in the curve of the earth around the sun; there is beauty in tilting wings against turquoise sky; there is beauty in the golden hue of wheat grass in amber light.

If we are to maintain the balance required to sustain life on earth, then our spiritual roots must grow deeper and wider.

SPIRITUAL ROOTS

"The great spirit, in placing men on the earth, desired them to take good care of the ground and to do each other no harm."

—*A Young Chief (1855)*
Cayuses

Native Americans cannot speak of religion without relating to the mountains, trees, sky and sun, plants and animals. Nor can they talk of nature without mentioning harmony, balance, reverence, beauty, and kinship. Nature is the embodiment of their spiritual beliefs. In the Native American psyche there is no separation of spirit, for the spirit dwells in all phenomena. It is their belief that in order to maintain a balance between the spiritual world and the physical world a "proper relationship" must be established between the two.

George Tinker (Osage)—*"A proper relationship recognizes that I am simply a part of creation, one of God's creatures along with other two-leggeds, the four leggeds, the wingeds, and other living, moving things—including the trees, the grass, the rocks, the mountains."*

Sing with Wolves)

Native American spirituality is tied to the land and runs deep and wide, connecting to the bones of their ancestors and all living, breathing, standing things. Modern mans' spiritual roots to the land, contrarily, are shallow and run vertically heavenward, instead of horizontally earthward. Because of our lack of earth-spirituality, we feel no compassion toward the other beings; no sense of responsibility for earth's well-being.

Listen to the cry of the Holy Wintu women as she describes the ruin of her homeland in a northern California forest during the 1800s—feel her deep-rooted compassion for the land and the trees. *"We do not chop down the trees. We use only dead wood. But the white people plow up the ground, pull down the trees, kill everything. The Tree says, 'Don't. I am sore.' But they chop it down and cut it up....The Indians never hurt anything, but the whites destroy all."*

Compassion for the land has all but been removed from the heart of modern society. We have lost our ability to feel the pain of earth as we live out our lives unaware of the spirituality of life about us.

Audrey Shenandoah (Onondaga)—*The Original Instructions that were given to us, direct that we who walk about the earth are to express a great respect, affection, and gratitude toward all the spirits who create and support life.*

If we are to maintain the balance required to sustain life on earth, then our spiritual roots must grow deeper and wider. We must elevate the way we envision ourselves in relation to our planet.

Sing with Wolves)

We do not have to invent a new belief system. We already have a draft. It is embedded in the ancient wisdom of the Native Americans. They do not speak of complex environmental laws to heal our ailing earth but merely to change the way we relate to our spirit-earth.

They speak with affection, the sacredness of our living planet. They advise us to rethink who we are as a humanity and to grow in earth-wisdom. They teach us that all phenomena are alive and full of spirit. They remind us that all life wishes to live without suffering and they warn that lack of respect for other living beings leads to a lack of respect for ourselves.

Once we restore our sensibilities for Mother Earth then the correct behavior in healing her will follow—politically, economically, socially, and spiritually.

We should realize by now—since the air we breath is fouled, the water we drink is poisoned, and the food we eat is cancerous—that we are not aliens from another galaxy but living members of a delicately balanced community on a planet called earth.

ALIENS

"Like winds and sunsets, wild things were taken for granted until progress began to do away with them. Now we must face the question whether a still higher standard of living is worth its cost in things natural, wild, and free."

—Aldo Leopold

We are not aliens from space to pilfer earth's riches and then leave the planet once the resources are diminished.

Earth is our home. Our only home. It is also home for the flowers that reach for the sun, snakes that shed their skin, and ducks that wade. We are one member among many sharing the same address.

We cannot leave our planet once we have made it inhabitable. And yet we are behaving as if we were aliens from another galaxy.

A short trip from my North Florida home are the beaches of the Gulf of Mexico. It is there that I am easily reminded of our alien attitude toward earth.

What was once a narrow ribbon of sugar-white sand dunes—home for scrub jays, beach mice, gopher tortoises, herons, and bald eagles—is now rapidly becoming leveled for vacation homes, resorts, golf courses, swimming pools, sea walls, steel fences, and signs saying, **"Keep Out Private Property."**

Sing with Wolves)

There are more beach-front-for-sale-signs than there are scrub jays and beach mice combined. It is a terrible sacrifice for the beach mouse and the scrub jay.

The Oklahoma land rush is still going on today. The dust tossed by racing horses, wagon wheels, and dreamy-eyed settlers has never settled.

The dust is still blowing in the wind only that it has now become toxic. If our pioneering spirit continues as it has, then mankind will be blowing in the wind.

If the pioneers were to stand trial among a jury of animal beings, they would probably be pardoned, if well behaved, by pleading ignorance.

Today however, we would probably get a life sentence for stupidity. As we enter the 21st century, stupidity is no excuse.

The pioneers had no ecological understanding of the land, although the Native Americans understood these concepts on a spiritual level.

We of the atom splitting, cyberspace and gene cloning age know very well that we are not dealing nature a fair hand. The cards at the moment are stacked against her.

In our alien frame of mind we do not want to share the earth.

We paint illusions in our heads, illusions of being independent of nature as we transfix our attention to acquiring material goodies. We refuse to give-up old models of living, models that say we are above all other living beings; the universe is nothing but a machine, and animals nothing more than soulless creatures.

Sing with Wolves 𝄆

Refusing to relinquish these old ideas only facilitates our quest to conquer and control, dominate and eradicate nature without feeling guilt, remorse, or responsibility—thus we have become aliens on our own planet. Because of our alien attitudes we are thinking only of ourselves and not of other earth beings.

We should realize by now—since the air we breath is fouled, the water we drink is poisoned, and the food we eat is cancerous—that we are not aliens from another galaxy but living members of a delicately balanced community on a planet called earth.

As I watch sand dune after sand dune fall prey to our selfish interests, I feel doubtful almost to the point of tears that earth can survive our obsessive demands.

Yet, there *is* a glimmer of hope. That hope lies in our willingness to recognize that other living beings are equally a part of our earth-community and our humbleness to admit our interdependence upon all that exists.

If we are to survive into the next millennium then we must consider what is good for other residents on earth. Before filling in a wetland, clear-cutting a forest or building a subdivision, we ask what is good for the heron nesting in the tree, the owl in the forest, the winged singer in the sedge. How can *we* survive without respecting other members of our earth-community? How can we respect ourselves?

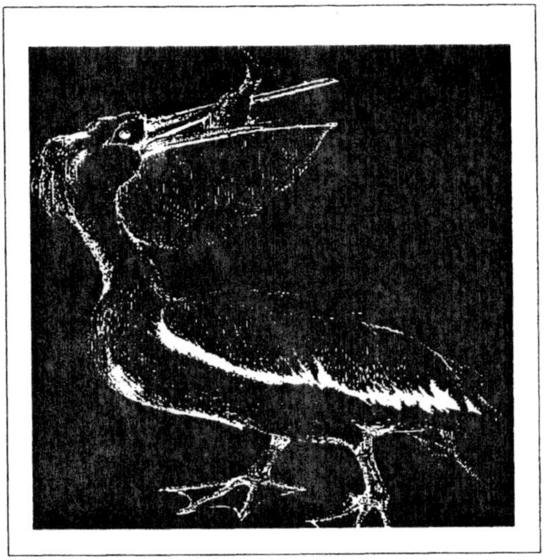

True power is coming upon a wildflower and admiring its beauty, then walking away empty handed. It is helping turtles across busy roads—braking for butterflies. This is the true power of the human being.

CROSSROADS
Red Road/Black Road

"Only within the moment of time represented by the present century has one species—man—acquired significant power to alter the nature of his world."

—Rachel Carson

Since the creation of the first iron tool, we have been bullying nature with our desire to control, conquer, subdue, and denude.

Finally we have tamed Mother Earth; we have controlled her rivers; we have conquered her mountain peaks; we have subdued her wild beasts; we have denuded her forests. The battle was long fought but now we can feel protected from the evils of wilderness, and enjoy the earth's treasures that is rightly ours.

We by far are superior beings, the center of the universe in which all the stars revolve. We can now stand atop her highest of craggy peaks and pound our hairy chest in victory.

Right?

Of course not!

If we must show our superiority then let us do so not by muscle-flexing or chest-thumping. This is not a sign of strength

Sing with Wolves 🌙

or superiority; it is a sign of weakness—let us show our strength by letting things live when we have the power to destroy, let us show affection when we have the capacity to harm, and let us show compassion when we have the tendency to bare our fangs.

True power is coming upon a wildflower and admiring its beauty, then walking away empty handed. It is helping turtles across busy roads—braking for butterflies. This is the true power of the human being.

According to the visionary minds of the Lakota Sioux, there are two symbolic roads in life, the black road (destruction) and the red road (the straight path).

The road we take whether it is black or red will direct the course of our life and life that has yet to unfold. We are always at the crossroads with every act and decision. Whatever road we take, that is our destiny.

At the crossroads we must decide what is not only beneficent for ourselves but what is beneficent for other living beings in which we share our maternal earth—the muskrat and the clam, the whale and the sea urchin, the butterfly and the moth, the tiger and the panda.

What is good for other plant and animal beings is also good for the human beings. Their welfare is our welfare, for we are all bound together in this great unfolding of life.

We are all dependent on clean air, pure water, and an array of living forms living out their purpose.

We can no longer afford to flex our muscles at nature. Nature is not the enemy; the enemy is within ourselves. Mother

Sing with Wolves

Nature can no longer compensate for our boldness.

We are at the final crossroads. We cannot risk taking another detour. The decision is ours alone.

Shall we listen to our heart and soul and take the red road or shall we continue listening to our whimsical ego that has painted illusions of largeness in our heads and desires the distance and the loneliness of the black road?

Red road or Black road? Love and compassion or domination and alienation?

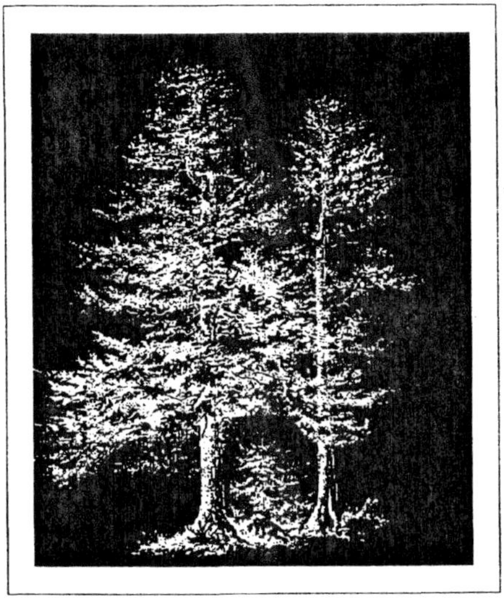

The human spirit requires close communion with nature. Thus, we journey to the dense forests, the mountain glens, and crooked canyons, not to conquer, but for peace and solitude, contemplation and self-renewal.

WILDERNESS

"Everybody needs beauty as well as bread, places to play in and pray in, where nature may heal and cheer and give strength to body and soul alike."

—John Muir *(1912)*

    Utah—*Just beyond the reach of lamp light, I walked to the edge of darkness. Tentacles of crooked light arched across the night sky, illuminating the buttes and mesas. As the storm closed-in, I watched the tumbled down wall of an ancient Anasazi dwelling light up and then disappear into the darkness. I could smell the rain coming my way. Just I was about to turn to camp I heard a startling cry that seemed to have leaped out of the darkness and crawled up my spine, shooting shock waves up to my heart. The cry was wicked; it was horrifying. I froze dead in my tracks. My self-serving-ego turn-tailed and hid behind my liver. Suddenly I was a mere human. Flesh and bone. Vulnerable and weak. I was no more or no less than the sidewinder or the cactus wren. I was a clumsy mannequin in the landscape of the mountain lion that screamed in the night.*

    Amidst the hum of laser printers, ringing phones, mountains of paperwork, meetings, deadlines and office protocol, I have, on many occasions, relived this comical event—that sacred moment in time. And when I do my slumbering soul awakens.

The point is, the human spirit requires close communion with nature. Thus, we journey to the dense forests, the mountain glens, and crooked canyons, not to conquer, but for peace and solitude, contemplation, and self-renewal. If wilderness dies, so does the human spirit.

Wallace Stegner—*Something will have gone out of us as a people if we ever let the remaining wilderness be destroyed, if we permit the last virgin forest to be turned into comic books and plastic cigarette cases; if we drive the few remaining members of the wild species into zoos or to extinction; if we pollute the last clear air and dirty the last clean streams and push our paved roads though the last of silence, so that never again will Americans be free in their own country from the noise, the exhausts, the stinks of human and automotive waste. And so that never again can we have the chance to see ourselves single, separate, vertical and individual in the world, part of the environment of trees and rocks and soil, brother to the other animals, part of the natural world and competent to belong in it.*

We moderns at times need to be jolted out of our common place and into a world of uncertainty. It is there in the loneliness of the wild that we can validate our finiteness as we gather up the stars and spin the moon.

Even if we never venture into the wild, it is good to know that such places unmolested by human endeavors still remain

Sing with Wolves 》

intact.

The wilderness is a sanctuary for weary spirits. It is a place we can go to restore our sensibilities—our mind, body, and spirit; it is sacred ground in which we can walk with the animal beings and talk to the plant beings; and listen to the voice of the wind.

The wilderness does not judge and has no prejudice. We are on equal footing with other wilderness beings, be it the squirrel or chipmunk, Douglas fir, or the desert primrose. It is there, beneath the forest canopy or deep inside the gaping earth that we can scream our heads off, shout profanities, or get naked and run wild through the forests, creeks and meadows or through brier patches if we desire.

In the wild there is no protocol.

It is a sanctuary where our spirits can soar among clouds scattered.

Henry Thoreau—*We need the tonic of wildness—to wade sometimes in marshes where the bittern and the meadow-hen lurk, and hear the booming of the snipe; to smell the whispering sedge whereonly some wilder and more solitary fowl builds her nest, and crawls with its belly close to the ground.*

Again, we have been misled to believe that wilderness, too, is something outside ourselves. And that is, perhaps, the root cause of the ruin of our precious wildlands.

Native Americans envisioned the wilderness as their mother. For she provided them food, clothing, medicine, and shelter.

Sing with Wolves)

Through prayer and ceremony, they expressed thanks for all that she provided. They understood that wilderness was equally the home to the animal beings and plant beings, the singing ones—all creatures of the wild.

We can no longer rob ourselves and others of the beauty and splendor of wild places by wantonly destroying it for greed and profit. These acts of violence are acts violence against ourselves.

John Muir—*Walk away quietly in any direction and taste the freedom of the mountaineer. Camp out among the grass and gentians of glacier meadows, in craggy garden nooks..."*

We must awaken from our foolish dream that we are separate from the wild. For we are not. We are inseparable.

We must enter the wilderness not as separate souls, but as universal beings. We must feel within our throbbing hearts love and compassion for all that is wild; to love the wild is to love the song of life—for the wild sings within us.

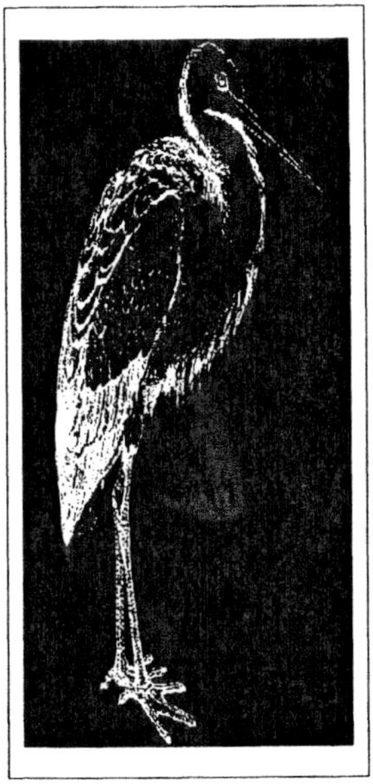

What would become of us if the last bird fell from the sky; the forests hushed; the streams lifeless—the yodel of the coyote unheard?

THE SEEING HEART

"What is life? It is the flash of a firefly in the night. It is the breath of the buffalo in the winter time. It is the little shadow that runs across the winter grassland and looses itself in the sunset."

Crowfoot (1800s)
Black Foot

We all have childhood memories of looking at the simple beauty in the world around us.

Flashbacks of our tender years are filled with memories of chasing fireflies in the night, wondering where rainbows ended, seeing whales and bears in passing clouds and building sandcastles in the sand.

We did not question the purpose of life, we just accepted it without challenge.

I can remember many sunny days as a child lying belly down on my lawn and viewing the world beneath the long slender blades of grass.

With a large magnifying glass held in my small hands, ants became as big as dinosaurs, grains of sand as big as boulders, and dragonflies and ladybugs were mystical creatures from fairy tales.

Sing with Wolves

All too often, as we grow into adulthood, we lose our childhood wonder for the natural world around us.

No longer are we spellbound by a starry night, or view the world upside down in a dewdrop.

Butterflies no longer intrigue us; chasing fireflies are all but a faded memory. The child dreamers we once were has all become a misty thought.

We have sacrificed spontaneity and wonderment for rigid goals. Worry instead of wonder becomes the main order of the day.

On our journey to adulthood we have been tutored that man is the center of the universe; nature is something outside ourselves.

We are taught to believe in the old wagon-wheel philosophy that there is plenty for all and that man is independent of all other living things.

As adults, we no longer dream of building sandcastles in the sand but homes where the gopher tortoise lives, golf courses in mountain valleys, ski resorts on sacred native land, shopping centers on wetlands.

In our haste to fulfill our dreams, we forget to ask what is good for the gopher tortoise who burrows in the sand, the great blue heron who nests in the big cypress, or the human spirit that yearns for places free and wild.

It is time to rid our minds of the belief that we are the center of the universe, that nature is something outside of us, something to be tamed, and something to be conquered.

Sing with Wolves)

As Lorean Eisley wisely stated: *"The need is not for more brains, the need is for a more tolerant people than those who won for us the ice age, the tiger, the bear."* Today our planet desperately needs a different kind of warrior, a warrior who feels compassion and awe for the natural world around him or her.

Naturalist John Muir exemplifies a true hero-warrior who never lost his child-like wonder for the natural world around him; he had a wonderful ability to transcend himself, becoming totally immersed in his surroundings.

Listen to his words as he describes the beauty of deer in an Oregon forest:

"Deer give beautiful animation to the forest, harmonizing finely in their color and movements with the gray and brown shafts of the trees and the swaying of the branches as they stand in groups at rest, or move gracefully and noiselessly over the mossy ground about the edges of beaver-meadows and flowery glades...."

In this poetic passage you can not help but feel the awe and wonderment Muir must have felt during this single moment.

Naturalist Henry David Thoreau was in a similar state of mind when he wrote:

"Sometimes as I drift idly along Walden Pond, I cease to live and begin to be."[1]

Sing with Wolves

Those who see with the heart have this wonderful ability to lose oneself in the moment, becoming that which is observed.

In order to see with the heart, we must banish the illusion of self-separateness and envision our existence as part of a greater whole.

The traditional Native Americans knew this well. They did not see themselves as apart from nature but a part of nature. They saw themselves as a part of the cycle of life.

Sacred rituals were performed to celebrate the season: the season of the seed, the season of collecting wild berries, the season of the harvest and the season of the hunt.

They recognized plants and animals as beings and called them brother and sister. And when they killed for food they gave thanks to the animal for giving up its life so that they may live. And when they died, they entered the sky as clouds and returned as rain.

The traditional Native Americans were warriors who lived by an ethic of balance, harmony, mutualism, and a sense of sacredness with the natural world around them.

Perhaps, we, of the industrialized societies would benefit by developing ethics, rituals and myths similar to that of the Native Americans.

Instead of worshipping books, perhaps we should worship the trees which made them; instead of worshipping fur coats, perhaps we should worship the animals from which their furs were stolen.

How often do we celebrate the plants and animals, the mountains and rivers, the forests, prairies, and deserts.

Sing with Wolves)

We must ponder our future without such an ethic.

What would become of us if the last bird fell from the sky; the forest hushed; the streams lifeless—the yodel of the coyote unheard? We may survive with only a few living things, tokens of what was once infinite possibilities, but we would only be half-living, for our spirits thirst for the wild, and our hearts would turn to stone.

I am, yet, reminded of another warrior type. A warrior who has not yet realized the beauty in the moment or the sacredness of life but sees the moment as opportunity and ceases the moment to conquer and to fulfill his manhood.

My thoughts return to Idaho, a cross-country ski trip, a mountain lion, and a warrior of yesteryear.

Except for the sound of swishing skis, all was silent. There were six of us gliding among the gentle foothills of Camas Prairie. Suddenly, the swishing stopped. We all stood frozen in our tracks, mesmerized by what we saw. It was a mountain lion. How graceful, fluid, and majestic this powerful animal appeared bounding over chest-high snow. We maintained our frozen postures until the mountain lion suffused into the blinding white horizon. The frigid air then cracked with laughter and joy. We all felt privileged to have witnessed such a rare and beautiful sight. I was so inspired by this encounter that I wrote a poem about the mountain lion.

Energy in motion / Fluid grace / Sprinting over glistening snow crystals / Power wound like tight chord / Unwinding / Flowing / Poetry in one swift motion.

Sing with Wolves

A week later, I happened upon a newspaper article that quickly saddened my heart. It was a front page article of a mountain lion shot near where we skied.

The article told the story of a warrior of yesteryear and how he saw the mountain lion drinking water at a creek and how he pulled his fierce weapon from his truck and shot the mountain lion dead.

A grisly photograph showed the old warrior with his rifle nestled proudly in his arm. Next to him was the mountain lion hanging from the rafter of his porch.

The newspaper article was slanted toward heroism instead of admonishment; bravery instead of cowardliness.

It is time for "a gentler, more tolerant people." The ice age is over; the west is won. Now is the moment for a new vision: a vision of sharing and mutual respect for all that lives.

May this new vision be a mountain in which we climb to insure that life on earth continues to unfold in all its complexity, beauty, and wonder.

The higher up the Mountain we climb the better humanity will become.

As our awareness of sacredness grows and our love and compassion for all life continues, we become warriors of a different sort. Not warriors wielding a sword against nature but warriors who see with the heart.

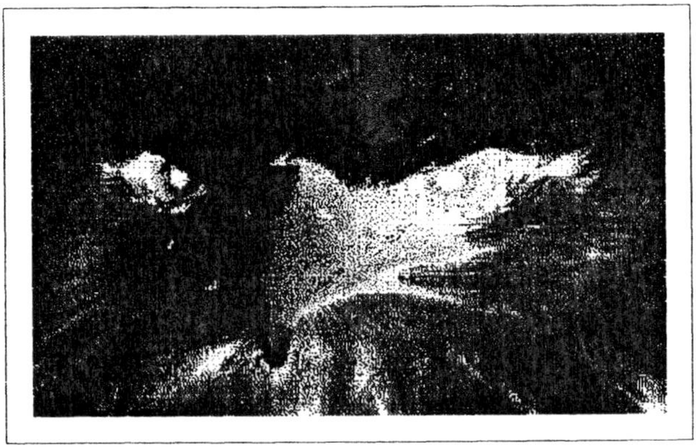

...the wolf teaches that there is strength in unity, the rabbit instructs that there is humility in quietness, the turtle advises to slow down and enjoy life.

Earth, Wind, and Sky

"Many animals have ways from which man can learn a great deal, even from the fact that horses are restless before a storm."

—Siya'Ka

Native Americans believe that animal beings are our teachers. The animal beings, they say, can teach us valuable lessons on the right way to live and think. For instance, the wolf teaches that there is strength in unity. The rabbit instructs that there is humility in quietness. The turtle advises to slow down and enjoy life.

Many summers ago, I had an eagle for a teacher. At that time, I did not know he was my teacher. My mind, then, was immature and was not ready to understand its teachings.

While I stood at the rim of Idaho's Snake River Canyon, I watched a spectacular rainbow after a sweeping storm. Then I noticed an eagle slice the sky with its broad wings. Below its belly was the—pea-green—Snake River, threading its way to the Columbia River. I watched the eagle's shadow stream across waves of blue-green sage and lichen covered stones. I

Sing with Wolves

watched him until nightfall.

Years later, the eagle flew into a dream. I could see him like it was yesterday—dipping and gliding carefree above the canyon. Like a flaming dart, the eagle dove below the rim, spiraling towards the river.

He kept like a dart until he hit the river. Then there was no eagle. Just river.

Suddenly I awoke and saw the blue moon spilling over my crumpled sheets. It was then that I understood the eagle's tongue. The eagle said, *"The rolling wind beneath my wings, yawning earth and flowing waters, blue-green sage, sunsets, clapping thunder, downpours and rainbow skies—I am all these things. I am the honored land given wings."*

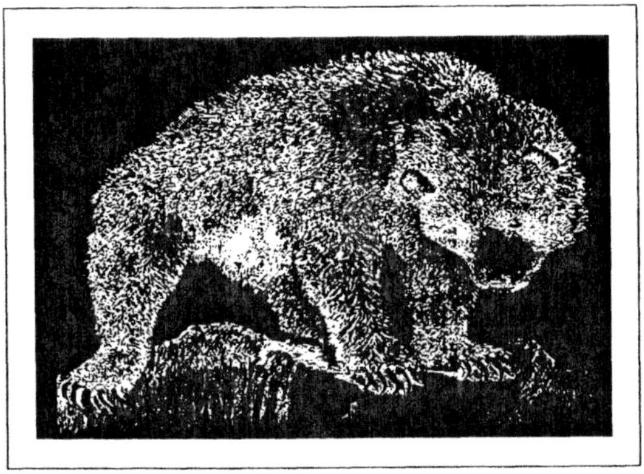

We have wondered to far from the cradle. It is time we return so that we may live in harmony with ourselves and other beings on our spirit-planet.

THE SPIRIT WITHIN

It is the story of all life that is holy and is good to tell, and of us two-leggeds sharing in it with the four-leggeds and the wings of the air and all green things; for these are children of one mother and their father is one spirit.

—Black Elk
Sioux Elder

    Occasionally we find ourselves alone in the dark, sandwiched between earth and cosmos. Inevitably, we grope for answers as to who we are in this vast forever expanding universe.

    As our imagination spirals outwards in quest for understanding, it soon recoils with a Snap!, frustrated and bewildered more than ever before. In a way, we are like orphans in space. We do not know where we came from, why we are here, or where we are going—all we know is that we exist on a spinning planet lush with life. From darkness we came and into the light we stepped. Beyond that lies another great mystery. Darkness→light→?

    Scientists tell us that our existence began not only on earth, but up there beyond the tree tops in the cradle of space. Everything, they teach, is made from atoms spewed forth from a great cosmic event 15 billion years ago—every flower, tree, stream, insect, and stone is sizzling with primordial cosmic

Sing with Wolves)

energy. The Native Americans confirm that we are a part of the universe, but they go a step further to tell us that we are not just a heap subatomic particles. They say there is a Great Spirit infused in all existence—every feather, leaf, and molecule is imbued with a spiritual essence.

Black Elk—*The first peace, which is the most important, is that which comes with the soul of people when they realize their relationship, their oneness, with the universe and all its powers, and when they realize that at the center of the universe dwells the Great Spirit, and that this center is really everywhere, it is within each of us.*

Cusp an earthworm in your hand and feel the spirit force wiggling within it; feel the drum of your heart or witness the magical budding of spring—it is the spirit force within.

Once this truth is embraced, no longer will we find ourselves baffled beneath a Goliath universe fishing for answers as to who we are. Peace instead of bewilderment, oneness instead of separateness will soak into us.

Mind, spirit and matter have always been One. It is only in our thoughts, the way we have conceptualized ourselves in relation to the world about us that we have become dissected from the rest of creation.

We have wandered too far from the cradle and it is time we return so that we may live in harmony with ourselves and other beings on our spirit-planet.

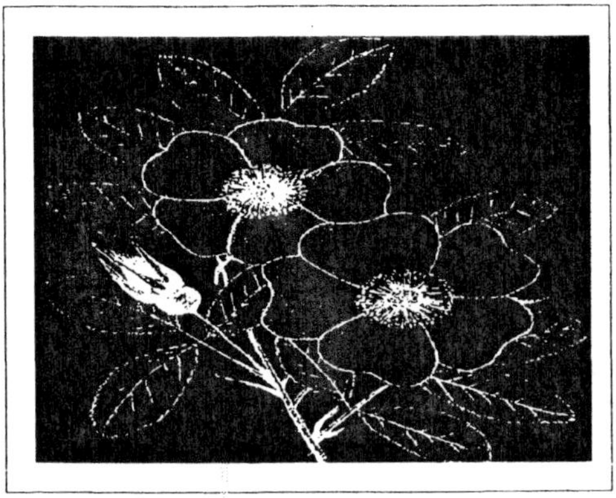

The creative power manifested all that exists. The creative power is what urges eggs to hatch, flowers to bloom, and caribou to migrate. It is the space between the notes of the mocking bird, frost in the meadow, and wind beneath bending wings.

SACRED MOMENTS

The mountains, I become part of it...The herbs, the fir tree, I become part of it. The morning mists, the clouds, the gathering waters, I become a part of it. The wilderness, the dew drops, the pollen...I become part of it.

—*Navajo Chant*

It's morning. Like steam from a witch's kettle, ghostly water vapors rise from the lake's tranquil surface. The sun is but a fuzzy orange behind the veil of fog.

A string of Canada geese pass overhead, undulating like musical notes on a staff, while an osprey whirls around the sun and a great blue heron stands frozen in a mat of bulrush.

I hear the brittle clash of leaves from a playful breeze, while observing a glint of sunlight on dragonfly wings.

I sip my coffee, now cooled, after a half-hour of watching the morning activities on Lake Tallavana, my Florida home.

Intuitively, intellectually, and philosophically, I feel that all life, whether it is an amoebae, an earthworm, aardvark or giraffe are spiritual creations.

For example, as I sit in complete silence, I am not passively

Sing with Wolves

observing the scenery. I do not merely see geese, an osprey, or a great blue heron in a lake scene with rising fog. I see them as spiritual beings. In a way I am having a spiritual experience.

Even the fog and the glint of sunlight on dragonfly wings is part of the spiritual feeling, including the breeze in the reeds. In some facet, I am connected to all that I experience on this beautiful morning.

The sun moves the wind; the wind ripples the water; the water bobs the geese—creating an emotion that sings a tune throughout my entire being. It is a beautiful symphony orchestrated by a Great spiritual force in the transitory moment.

Brave Buffalo—*When I was ten years of age I looked at the land and the rivers, the sky above, and animals around me and could not fail to realize that they were made by some great power. I was so anxious to understand this power that I questioned the trees and bushes. It seemed as though the flowers were staring at me. Then I had a dream, and in my dream one of these small round stones appeared to me and told me that the maker was Wanka Tanka, and to honor him I must honor nature.*

The creative power manifested all that exists and is all that exists; it is what urges eggs to hatch, flowers to bloom and caribou to migrate; it is the space between the notes of the mocking bird, frost in the meadow, dew on grass—wind beneath bending wings.

Sing with Wolves)

I have often lost my sense of Self while photographing nature, watching a sunset, listing to the gurgle of a mountain stream or just about anywhere that I choose to fine tune my attention and open my heart.

I become thirsty as a sponge soaking up the beauty and the magic of the moment—absorbed in inner peace and contented as a child making mud pies.

David Cavagnaro, must have had a similar experience as in this passage from his book, "Feathers."

"I have become an eagle. I have known the mountains and have seen with his eyes the vastness and the majesty of this earth. I have soared through thunderheads, pursuing the setting sun, and have fallen gently earthwards as a single feather shed in the depths of a star-filled night. As the feather of an eagle, I have known lightness and strength; I have danced in the sacred dances; I have known the meaning of beauty."

To know the meaning of beauty is to cast away our beliefs of self-separateness from the natural world. We must come out of our skin and become one—in spirit—with that which we see.

We must learn to cross over into that other dimension in which the *I* of me ceases to be.

In so doing, we may find ourselves, more often than not, suspended in a fleeting moment—entranced at the water's edge—observing a frog jumping into the moon or finding our beating hearts in rhythm of each wing-swoop of a passing gull.

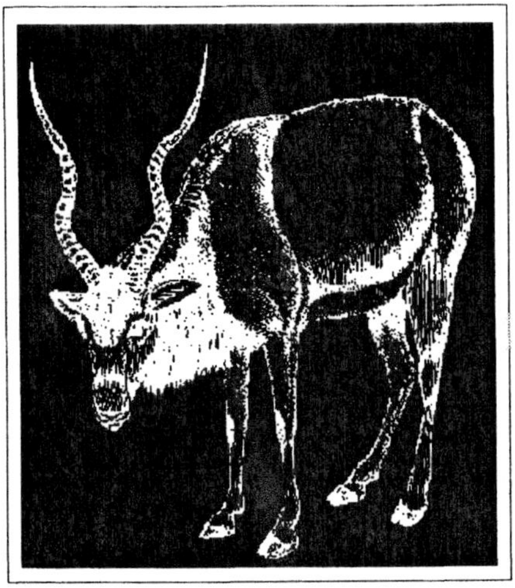

Without purpose, planets, moons, stars, and whole galaxies would fling apart, geese would cease to migrate, water would flow uphill, clouds wouldn't rain, flowers wouldn't bloom.

PURPOSE

"Any object has the right to exist, simply because it has its own being, its own history, its own motive and purpose.

—John Muir

All life has purpose. The purpose of an acorn is to become an oak tree, an egg a soaring hawk, the nymph a mayfly, and man a compassionate being toward all existence.

All life has the right to fulfill its purpose.

The caterpillar has the right to become a butterfly, and the tadpole a frog. Each living thing by fulfilling it purpose contributes to the greater whole.

No longer must we see other living things as simply non-thinking or impulsive creatures but unique living beings living out their lives with cause.

It is because many things have purpose and are carrying out that purpose that life in all its complexity, exists.

Without purpose, planets, moons, stars, and whole galaxies would fling apart, geese would cease to migrate, water would flow uphill, clouds wouldn't rain, flowers wouldn't bloom.

By cultivating such an awareness we become sensitive to the

natural wonders around us. Instead of plucking a flower because we desire its beauty, we bend low and admire its beauty, desiring to let it live and to fulfill its purpose.

In our progressive high-tech society of diminishing resources, fractured ecosystems and mass species extinction, shouldn't we be more appreciative of the purpose of other living things?

When we see other beings living with intention, then our perspective of the natural world around us changes.

Poet Gwen Frostic—*Life begins with beauty and promise...it must fulfill that promise or perish along the way.*

We, too, must fulfill our promise—to become more compassionate for other living beings. If not, then we too shall *perish along the way.*

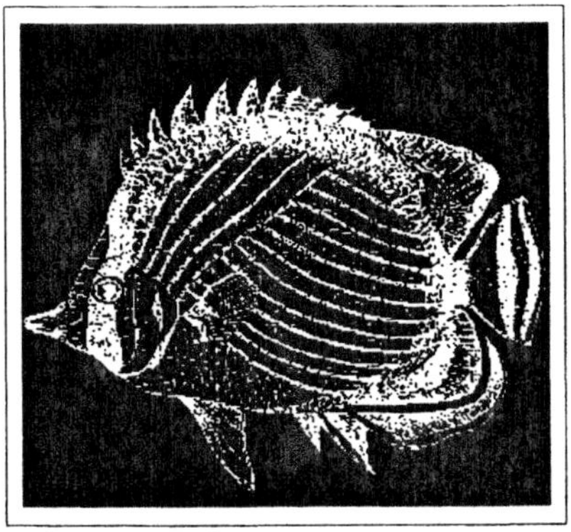

If we would awaken to the daily beauty of nature, then we would soon discover a simple truth—heaven is all around us.

SACRED BEAUTY

"Those who contemplate the beauty of the earth find reserves of strength that will endure as long as life."

—Rachel Carson

How odd, on a planet that is so heaped in beauty, we, the human beings, are so blind of earth's sublimity. Why is it that we humans, gifted with an awareness that life is not only a rarity but is a one time deal, are not rejoicing.

Edward Abbey—*How strange and wonderful is our home, our earth, with its swirling vaporous atmosphere, its flowing climbing creatures, the croaking things with wings that hang on rock, and soar through fog, the furry grass, the scaly seas...How utterly rich and wild...Yet some among us have the nerve, the insolence, the brass, the gall to whine about the limitations of our earthbound fate, and yearn for some more perfect world beyond the sky.*

We walk blindly through life as if our time on earth could flood a sea. In truth, our time on earth could not fill a thimble.

Sing with Wolves)

We have chosen *not* to see the beauty of our living earth but to walk swiftly through it. We dream of a surreal place somewhere beyond the clouds in which someday we will journey.

During our cloud-dreaming we fail to notice earth's sacred beauty. Afterall, why should we pay attention to earth when eventually we will take residence up there beyond the ionosphere, beyond the most distant galaxies.

If we would open our eyes to the daily beauty of nature, then we would soon discover a simple truth—heaven is all around us. Like ice and snowflakes heaven and earth are inseparable.

We too are inseparable from earth. For we are made of shifting continents and ancient seas and worn-down mountains. The spirit-force weaves through us. Thus, we are intimately joined with all creation. For all creation is of One-Spirit!

Black Elk—*We should know that all things are the works of the Great Spirit. We should know that He is within all things: the trees, the grasses, the rivers, the mountains, and all the four-legged animals, and the winged peoples; and even more important, we should understand that He is also above these things and peoples.*

When our sense of earth-spirituality is deeply rooted in our thoughts, we can begin to understand that the depth of our being extends far beyond the boundaries of our limited perceptions.

By developing a sense of earth-spirituality, we find ourselves more often than not, dazzled by the awesome beauty and mystery of life about us; a new sense of peace and calm envelopes us. We find ourselves caring about the welfare of our ailing planet and supporting programs that protects wildlife and ecosystems.

Albert Schweitzer—*Life outside a person is an extension of the life within him. This compels him to be part of it and accept responsibility for all creatures great and small.*

We are one in the same with all creation. As we begin to understand this truth we will see the unexpected beauty in all of life's spiritual intertwinings and come to realize for the first time that the beauty of life around us is also a reflection of the beauty within.

ENDNOTE

Every since we left the cold and clammy confines of our cave dwellings and sought a better means of insulating ourselves from the moods of earth, we have isolated ourselves from our outer-half—nature. We have cocooned ourselves with pink insulation, sheet rock, and tiled roofs to the extent that we have been superficially convinced that we are in some quirky way, separate from the world outside our double pain windows. In our quest to make our lives more comfortable, we have all but forgotten our earth-connection.

We have arrived at the point, it seems, that we do not care about anything outside our own earthly desires. We have fallen prey to our insatiable hunger for having, instead of being. To be materially rich is by far more important than being spiritually fulfilled.

Sing with Wolves)

Are We Better Off?

Our trust in technological wizardry to provide us with a fulfilling life has failed. Mass consumerism has become our fatal attraction. There are millions of us who have all the goodies in life who are suffering from a deep sense of emptiness—an emptiness of the heart and spirit. We often find ourselves alone and pondering, 'Is this all there is to life?' Even in our sleep thoughts of despair rustle in our heads like leaves caught in a whirlwind. We must ask ourselves some basic questions—Has our technological success made us any happier? Is pirating global ecosystems to satisfy our material glut worth wrecking our planet?

Turning Our Backs On Mother Earth

For so long we have turned our backs on Mother Earth. Now is the season to give Mother Earth back to herself. We must give back her mountains so that they may in return give back themselves to the bear and the lynx. We must give back her streams so that they may in return give back themselves to the salmon and the trout. We must give back her forests so that they may in return give back themselves to the wolverine and the fox. When we give Mother Earth back to herself, we give back her dignity and we enhance our humanity.

Sing with Wolves I

Within the past 100 years, scientists estimate over a million species have become extinct. Mostly as a result of our taking away their homescape—their livelihood. Ninety percent of our nation's wetlands are gone! Ninety percent of the Pacific Northwest ancient forests—destroyed! Fifty percent of our tallgrass prairies—lost forever. All have vanished because of human activity.

As of yet, it seems, we are not willing to give nature back to Mother Earth. We are still resistant in giving up our spoils. We are even willing to continue to tolerate breathing toxic air, and drinking polluted water for the sake of maintaining our material pursuits. Millions of metric tons of pollutants are still being injected into the atmosphere, marine estuaries, and the land each year.

We Humans Are A Paradox

We have been blessed with a melon-size brain that has catapulted us from the stone age to the space age in a relatively short period. No other creature is capable of transcribing thoughts into symbols, symbols into works of art, literature, poetry, and song. Beneath the burning stars we have been gifted with an intelligence that can ponder the reality of our own existence. Yet, apparently, we have not yet developed the wisdom or maturity to stay out of trouble—to live in harmony with the natural world that sustains us. We are like infants with a flaming match in one hand and a firecracker in the other, not realizing the consequences of our actions.

Has Mother Nature Goofed?

It has been suggested that we human beings are not, perhaps, fully human. Maybe we are prehuman. This could be since the human being has only been evolving for a mere 3 million years or so. Three million years hardly registers on the geological time clock. And yet, here we are an infant species that has developed the ability to crack open atoms, tinker with genes, and destroy every living being on earth.

Has mother nature giving birth to a runaway child? If there is going to be a future for humanity, then we must learn to tame *not* nature but our intellect and to relearn to listen to our heart. Without all there is, there would be no life. Our talking heart is telling us that this is the true path of our unfolding—to honor all life.

Earth From Afar

Above my computer desk hangs a picture of earth. It was taken by astronauts during the Apollo 17 voyage to the moon.

Sing with Wolves)

We are all familiar with this photograph—the swirling white clouds beneath which lies the horse-head continent of Africa and the startling blue Mediterranean Sea against a backdrop of coal-black space. This photograph is a powerful symbol to remind me of my place in the cosmos:

- *It is to remind me that the earth is round, therefore, is limited. It can support so many plants, animals, birds, fish, and people.*

- *It is to remind me to walk lightly and to live simply so that others may live. The more I take for myself, the less there is for others.*

- *It is to remind me that living on earth is a relationship. It is a relationship between you and me, plants and animals, water and air.*

- *It is to remind me that earth is where I was born. It is where I live and there is no other planet like it in a billion solar systems.*

Challenging Our Beliefs

If we are to mend our broken spirits and heal our hurting earth, then we must rekindle our sense of kinship with her. With the widespread destruction of the earth's biosphere, is it not time we challenge our old assumptions about who we are on our home-planet?

Feeling a sense of kinship with earth and all her inhabitants can spring forth many positive changes in ourselves while healing our sick planet.

- *A sense of kinship creates a deep awareness of the woes of Mother Earth. Her suffering becomes our suffering.*

- *Increases our willingness to protect our living earth. We join environmental organizations that support our cause. We become politically active in supporting legislation that protect and preserve our living planet.*

- *Develops a sense of sacredness. When we envision earth as a sacred planet, we then develop a sense of reverence for all living beings. That which we revere we are less likely to harm.*

- *Leads to self-respect and an enlivened sense of purpose.*

For too long we have orphaned ourselves from our home in space. It is time to come home. It is time to seek a spiritual reunion with Mother Earth and all her citizens.

It is time to say goodbye to old beliefs of self-separateness from the natural world. It is time to celebrate our relatedness to all that exists. The time is now to step out of our makeshift

Sing with Wolves)

cocoons and into the sweet breath of the green world and humble ourselves among all earth's wondrous creations.

To heal our earth, we must love her with unending compassion. We can not love a part of her without loving the whole, for all things are intertwined in the great weaving of creation. We cannot love the eagle without loving the sky; we cannot love the wolf without loving the wilderness; we cannot love whales without loving the oceans. To love the trees is to love the forests.

Mother Earth Our Healer

If we help heal Mother Earth, she will help heal ourselves. In the ancient forests of the Pacific Northwest, *toxol* in the bark of the Pacific yew tree is now used to treat ovarian and breast cancer. Compounds in the rosy periwinkle, a flowering plant, are used to treat childhood leukemia. The purple foxglove, another flowering plant, contains the drug *digitalis* and is used to curtail heart attacks. She can also mend our broken spirits by bending light into multifarious colors after a sweeping storm, or provide us with the uplifting melody of a songbird—sent to us on a gentle breeze.

However, protecting our planet for the sole purpose of our

well-being is shallow and self-serving. Our desire to heal Mother Earth must come from the heart—simply for the love of all creation. For the joy of living comes from the knowing that we share a common bond with all that is.

INDEX TO QUOTATIONS

The Tattered Web
Chief Luther Standing Bear (pg. 20)—"Touch the Earth"- A Self Portrait of Indian Existence, Compiled by T.C. McLuhan. Copyright 1971 by T.C. McLuhan. Published by Promontory Press.

Alex Jacobs (Pg. 21)—from "The Way of the Earth: Encounters with Nature In Ancient And Contemporary Thought" Copyright 1994 by T.C. McLuhan, A Touch Stone Book, Published by Simon & Shuster.

Aldo Leopold (Pg. 22)—Quoted in "Wisdom of the Elders: Sacred Native Stories of Nature" Copyright 1992 by David Suzuki, Published by Bantam Books, A Division of Bantam Double Day Dell Publishing Group, Inc.

Dreamwalking
John Muir (Pg. 25)—from "Wilderness Essays" Copyright 1980, Peregrine Smith Books.

Edward Abbey (Pg. 13)—from "Earth Prayers." Edited by Elizabeth Roberts and Elias Amidon. Copyright 1991. Printed by Harper San Francisco, a division of Harper Collins San Francisco.

Spiritual Roots
A Young Chief (Pg. 31)—"The Way of the Earth."
George Tinker (Pg. 31)— Ibid.
Holy Wintu Women (Pg. 32) Ibid.
Audrey Shanandoah (Pg. 32) Ibid.

Aliens
Aldo Leopold (Pg. 37)—from "Earth Prayers."
Crossroads
Rachel Carson (Pg. 43)—From "Silent Spring"
Wilderness
Wallace Stegnar (Pg. 28)—Quoted in "Living Water" by David Cavagnaro and Frans Lanting. Copyright 1982 by Graphic Arts Center Publishing Company, Portland, Oregon.

Henry David Thoreau (Pg. 30)—from "The Thoughts of Thoreau" Edwin Way Teale Library of Classics. Copyright 1962 by Edwin Way Teale. Reissued 1987 by Dodd, Mead & Company, Inc.
The Seeing Heart
Crowfoot (Pg. 55)—Quoted in "Touch the Earth" Copyright by T.C. McLuhan 1971, Published by Promontory Press.

Lorean Eisley (Pg. 57)—Quoted in "The Living Water"

John Muir (Pg. 57)—Quoted in "John Muir, Wilderness Essays" Copyright 1985, 4th printing, by Gibbs M. Smith, Inc.
Earth, Wind, and Sky
Siya'ka (Pg. 63)—Quoted in "Animals of the Soul," by Joseph Epes Brown, copyright 1997 by Element Books Inc.
The Spirit Within
Black Elk (Pg. 67)—Quoted in "The Way of the Earth"

Black Elk (Pg. 68)—Ibid.
Sacred Moments
Navajo Chant (Pg. 69)—Quoted in "Earth Prayers"

Brave Buffalo (Pg. 70)—Quoted in "Touch the Earth - A Self Portrait of Indian Existence, Compiled by T.C. McLuhan. Copyright 1971 by T.C. McLuhan. Published by Promontory Press.

David Cavagnaro (Pg. 71)—From "Living Water"
Purpose
Jack Davis—"The Way of the Earth"

Gwen Frostic (Pg. 76)—From "Beyond Time" Copyright 1971, Presscraft Papers Inc., Benzonia Michigan.

Sacred Beauty

Rachel Carson (Pg. 79)—Taken from the U.S. Fish & Wildlife Service Web Page.

Edward Abbey (Pg. 79)—From "Earth Prayers"

Black Elk (Pg. 80)—Quoted in "The Way of the Earth."

Albert Schweitzer (Pg. 81)—Quoted in "The Soul of the Wolf: A Meditation on Wolves and Man" Copyright 1980 by Michael W. Fox.